It's Neat to Eat

By

Betty Page

Illustrated by Phil Wallace

AuthorHouse™
1663 Liberty Drive
Bloomington, IN 47403
www.authorhouse.com
Phone: 1-800-839-8640

First published by AuthorHouse   9/29/2011

ISBN: 978-1-4567-4174-7

Printed in the United States of America

Any people depicted in stock imagery provided by Thinkstock are models,
and such images are being used for illustrative purposes only.
Certain stock imagery © Thinkstock.

This book is printed on acid-free paper.

authorHOUSE®

Created by Betty Page

and

dedicated to Gerry Page and the Family

Illustrated by

Phil Wallace

If I could reach and catch a star,
I'd probably drop my candy bar.

Know what I could eat with ease?
A chewy, gooey, warm grilled cheese.

Jell-O, Jell-O we can't bake.
So we can't have a Jell-O cake.

Syrup, syrup really does worry.
It always seems in such a hurry.

Eating your veggies, like string beans,
might give you happy nighttime dreams.

Cookies shouldn't have to stay
hidden in their cookie tray.

Think, think, think again hard.
Suppose there were ice pops growing in the yard.

I'm glad I'm one and not a bunch.
I'd hate to share my hot dog lunch.

Pasta, pasta everywhere.
Even pasta in my hair.

How to stop a child from yell'un?
Mother feed him watermel'un.

When it's cold outside and the snow blows 'round,
chocolatey hot chocolate tastes best going down.

I cannot, cannot tell a lie.
I'm in love with pizza pie.

Apple, banana, pear or grape?
Oh, so many which should I take?

Do you like butter? I do too.
If we didn't have butter what would Mr. Bread ever do?

I like ice cream, I like candy.
I don't like them when they're sandy.

If I pretend they're little trees
that helps me eat my broccoli-eees.

Catsup, catsup pays no mind.
It either runs or stays behind.

Happy girls, happy guys,
when they're eating their French fries.

Oatmeal isn't a special, SPECIAL TREAT.
It's sloppy and droppy but kinda neat.

Peanut butter I think is swelly
spes'ly when it's with red jelly.

Soup is good, soup is yummy.
And it sure does warm your tummy.

Sometimes at night I lie awake
just thinking about my birthday cake.

You have finished the book; now I have a wish.

You make up a rhyme about your favorite dish.

CPSIA information can be obtained
at www.ICGtesting.com
Printed in the USA
253561LV00001B